Bullied

By

André "Dre" Cooper

Street Dreamz presents
BULLIED

ISBN-13: 978-0692485088 (Street Dreamz Publications)

ISBN-10: 0692485082

(For bulk orders, contact the author personally at his Facebook page andrecooper/chester.pa or go to midnightexpressbooks.com)
On all bulk order purchases, a portion of the proceeds will go to charities helping efforts to stop bullying.

Self-published with help from
MIDNIGHT EXPRESS BOOKS
POBox 69
Berryville AR 72616
(870) 210-3772
MEBooks1@yahoo.com

Also by the author

Hip-Hop Fiction Books

      The Life We Chose*

      The Life We Chose 2*

      Betrayal of Sinners*

*These books were written under the pen name of 'Dre'.

For Mom-Mom with love...

Rest in Peace.

We miss you dearly.

CHAPTER 1

Two huge windows lined the sidewall facing the main street which brought forth light rays of the autumn sun on the crowded classroom. Thirty students sat attentive while their English teacher gave a lecture on how to properly organize your thoughts into a paragraph.

The brown-skin boy squirmed a little in his seat, not enough to draw any attention to himself, but just enough to let any onlookers know that he *really* had to go. Cory glanced at the clock that sat above the white vinyl board where his teacher was writing an example for the class. She had just completed the second sentence then turned to speak. "Now..." Cory had his hand already raised which caused Ms. Benson to stop speaking in mid-sentence. "Yes, and I hope it's a question about grammar, Mr. Smith."

Gloria Benson was a young woman in her late thirties and dressed like it to. Not to flashy or tight fitting clothes, but teacher appropriate with an emphasis on being moderate. Ms. Benson wore a simple white blouse and black skirt that came slightly above her knees with black shoes. She loved children, as if they were her own. Therefore, she addressed her students with respect. Even though at times she felt that it was not grooming them properly for the real world because once they left her class other students, teachers and even parents addressed them in more degrading ways. She still tried her best to be an example for them to follow.

"No, ma'am but I have to use the bathroom very bad. I've been holding it since the beginning of class."

"Well, can you hold it a few minutes longer? This information will be on your test next week and it's only a couple minutes left before the class is over."

"No, Ms. Benson... My stomach is already hurting now from holding it this long."

None of the kids looked, laughed, or cared, if Cory was about to pee on himself.

"Okay, but make sure you get the information from somebody in the class... It's important Mr. Smith."

Cory snatched his things off the desk and grabbed his backpack off the floor, then shoved everything inside. He walked out of the room. Cory hurried down to his locker. Time was ticking away. School would end in ten minutes, but Cory needed a head start. He had been doing this exact routine for two weeks. Nobody noticed though except his friend, who also was running. By the classes rotating every day, he pulled the same stunt on all of his teachers when it was the last period of school.

Cory made it to his locker. He scanned both ways of the hall, then with the precision of a master locksmith, dialed the numbers and yanked the lock off and opened the locker. Cory tossed his backpack inside and grabbed his jacket and hat. He closed the locker back to secure all of his things inside. Cory waited a few seconds then snatched his cell phone out of his jacket pocket. He glanced at the screen. It read: October 28, 2014 at 3:10 pm. There were no missed calls, nor was he about to call anybody during school hours. Cory just needed to know how much time was left before school let out.

"Five minutes... Darn!" He said out loud to nobody but himself. Cory began to speed-walk down the basement hallway. The place was empty at this time of the day because classes were still being conducted. Orange lockers ran down both sides of the long hall with thin cheap black carpet covering the floor. The carpet stretched from one door, that lead to a stairway which could take you up to the third floor, main entrance and second and first floors. While, the doors leading to a stairway closes to Ms. Benson class on the right, could do the same but it also had a side door that exited to the teacher parking lot.

The lanky boy stood 5'5 and weighed 100 pounds, so he barely made a sound passing the numerous eighth grade classrooms that were visible between the lockers filling the walls. He reached the staircase without an incident, but didn't enter it yet. Cory looked at his phone again. It read: 3:13pm. He stepped in the stairway with caution. The hall was usually occupied by other kids who ditched class. This was also the bullies, drug dealers and cigarette smokers domain. It was off limits to most for the simple reason that it was not frequented by the school's security guard or teachers during the day except for when the teachers arrived to work in the morning. The school held twenty-five hundred students between the grades 8 through 12. The one guard couldn't cover that much area. Especially in the basement area where most of the vulnerable bunch of kids were placed.

Cory was confused by nobody being present today. It was always somebody hanging on the steps waiting to bully a kid, for no reason; shooting dice, making out with a girl or waiting on their friend to help sneak them back in school. But, Cory was more confused today with the fact that his friend Taron wasn't waiting for him as planned.

He couldn't wait any longer. The bell would ring any second and he needed a head start to make it home today. Cory pushed the door open and stepped out. No sooner as he was fully out of the side door, the bell went off notifying everybody that another day had ended. Cory took off running up the sidewalk.

The day was sunny, no wind and the October chill hadn't kicked in yet. The weather was still warm enough to wear just a thick sweatshirt without a jacket, but Cory didn't bother. It had been chilly earlier in the morning when him and Taron walked to school.

He dashed past the lined buses parked by the curb that hid the parking lot. Some of the more observant bus drivers looked at him and laughed. They knew what he was up to. A few of them had noticed his frequent pattern of darting past them every day for the past two weeks. Cory turned right, still passing the buses and ran up 9th Street in front of the school. He dashed pass the sign, poking out of the ground, that read, "Welcome to Chester High School-Class of 2014," and continued on pass the lady crossing guard. She didn't bother to help him cross the street or say anything about violating the school rules. He made a right at the next corner and ran all the way down to the end and turned left. Cory didn't stop. He headed past Earl's Funeral Home. When he reached Chester's famous track and football field, 8th field, Cory stopped running, but started speed walking.

He was out of danger for the moment. Cory's round face and small mouth was covered with drops of sweat and his chest heaved fast. He remained alert though. He was also most there. The Bennett Homes Housing Project was in full view. Each step he took brought a great chance of him making it.

CHAPTER 2

The end of school was a relief for most. After the long classes on different subjects some boring and others not worth attending, due to the overcrowded classes and uncommitted teachers and students not willing to learn, they couldn't wait for the last period of the day.

At the sound of the last bell, students flooded the hallways and stairways. Everybody was rushing to leave the place. Some needed to aboard the waiting buses outside, while others were hurrying to catch a ride home by friends and some like Taron were trying to make it past the bullies without being harmed.

Taron was a little kid. He stood no taller than five foot and weighed a 100 pounds soaking wet. This was Taron's first year at the school, as well as the other 8th graders first. Their regular schools had been closed down due to financial issues and the city's lack of interest in helping the youth. This lack of funding and help affected not only the schools, but the already poverty-stricken kids. Nobody cared that by placing such young kids around these older ones that it could make the younger kids prey to physical and mental abuse. Along with peer-pressuring issues.

It was the same story growing up in Taron's home. He was fatherless. Abuse was a regular thing growing up around two older brothers and sisters. Taron's mother was the only one, who tried to show him some type of love and compassion but she couldn't be around all the time so that left the door open for his brothers and sisters to abuse him. Taron never fought back though and was scolded and rejected by his family for being a weakling or soft as they called him. This label bothered Taron, but he didn't show it. He kept his feelings bottled up and tried to shrug off the beatings, as if he was the one that had done something wrong to earn the whipping.

He moved through the crowd of boys wearing yellow short-sleeve shirts and navy blue khaki pants. This was the school's standard dress. Everybody had to wear the same outfits except the girls. They wore yellow short-sleeve shirts with navy blue pleaded skirts. Taron reached his locker. He peaked around before unlocking it. Taron was trying to stay focused and get out of the way of the other kids. He unlocked the locker and grabbed a few books and placed them in his backpack. Taron closed the locker and headed towards the stairway that lead to the parking lot. He didn't want to take the other route even though it might have been safer. More teachers would be standing around outside their classes. Other students would be moving about in the main hallway heading out the front entrance of the school. But, Taron decided against it. That was the same way he took when he was caught last time.

Instead of waiting inside the school, they waited outside across the street from the school behind some buses. Taron couldn't see them, but as he walked in between the buses they spotted him. He continued to head their way and prayed that they wouldn't bother him. Taron was wrong. He got pass several of the boys, who were making jokes and laughing at him for showing fear which they noticed by his demeanor and failure to look at them or walk with his head up. The boys followed Taron. He walked at a fast pace hoping that he wouldn't be harmed. Out of nowhere, Taron felt something like a little rock hit him in the back of the head. He didn't stop or turn around to see who threw it. It didn't matter to him. He wasn't going to stand up for himself. Taron just reached back and rubbed his head. At the time, Taron sported a Mohawk hairstyle. He was dark-skinned with curly black hair, so he liked to wear it out, especially when a pretty girl in the ninth grade told him to do so. Taron tried to pull the rock out and noticed that it was stuck to his hair. The boy had tossed a chewed up piece of gum at him and it tangled in Taron's Mohawk. The five boys laughed hard then ran up on Taron. They circled him. The biggest one out of the group stepped up to Taron. He was a 10th grader and from one the dangerous areas in Chester - Highland Gardens.

The neighborhood was located on the Westside and known to be violent. There were incidents that took place inside of the place where kids got shot and even a couple kids, no older than thirteen, had killed their ice cream truck driver, who had been serving them for years, in an apparent robbery attempt.

Taron stopped dead in his tracks when Tom-Tom stood in front of him. Tom-Tom stared at him and then, with an open hand, smacked Taron hard across his slim face. Tom-Tom stood the same size as Taron, but weighed 40 pounds more. Taron fell back a little. He faked as if he was going to run to the left, but darted to the right. The quick fake and strong first step of Taron caught the boys off guard. At first, nobody tried to chase him until they saw Tom-Tom take off running after him. They all followed, but Taron was turning the corner by then. Tom-Tom and the others chased him for several blocks before stopping. Taron made it safely to his housing project that day and thanked God for not getting caught.

Taron didn't want to repeat that incident. It had been a close call. Just like that day, Cory had left school before him. Today wasn't any different. Cory failed to wait for Taron after class again. They had made a pact that they would not leave each other again, but Cory broke the promise and left him today. It wasn't on purpose, Taron thought. It couldn't be.

He scanned the area looking for the band of wild boys. As usual, they were nowhere around on the basement level. They got hip to most of the kids tactics of avoiding them. So, every day after school, they hurried and stood on the side streets around the area of the school. They got smarter and started picking different spots each day to wait on their prey. Tom-Tom and them picked on the loners or those boys who were unpopular and not associated with any of the different hoods in the city. They took money, clothes and the courage of the boys.

Taron walked to the staircase, but was slightly bumped before going in by a petite dark chocolate girl coming through the doors.

"Excuse me!" She said with a bright smile. Aisha had been keeping an eye on Taron since they met on the first day of school.

She was a 9th grader, cheerleader and hung with all the popular girls in school.

"It's cool... How you been doing?"

"I'm good... Why haven't you called me?" Aisha got straight to the point. She pumped herself up all day to say that to him.

Taron smiled at the question.

"What? ... You not trying to be my friend?" She asked with a childlike sassy tone, then placed a hand on her hip.

Taron was surprised by her aggressive manner.

"No, it ain't that... I lost your number and kept forgetting to ask you for it."

"Boy, stop lying... I come down here every day to see you... Why you didn't ask me for the number again?"

"I keep forgetting."

Aisha wasn't taking no for an answer. She went into her backpack and grabbed a pen. Aisha snatched Taron's hand, then wrote her number down. "Now, you got it... Make sure you call me tonight or else I'm going to beat you up tomorrow boy." She chuckled at the remark. "Matter of fact, where ya phone at?"

Taron reached into his blue khakis and grabbed his phone. Aisha snatched it out of his hand. She started rummaging through his numbers then called her phone. Aisha reached back inside her bag and picked up her own phone. It was vibrating lightly, as the phone kept ringing. She handed Taron back his phone and accepted the call. "Got it... Hold up. Smile!"

Taron blushed when she lifted her phone to take a flick.

"I got it." Aisha scanned the picture then stored it.

"Darn, Aisha I wasn't even ready to take a picture."

"Boy you good... And, I'm storing it in my phone under... My boo!"

"Stop playing girl..."

"Look!" She showed him the picture. He tried to snatch it, but she yanked it back. "So, I better not see you talking to any of these girls around here because me and you about to go together... Aight?" She stared at him with her face twisted slightly trying to catch his reaction.

Taron just smiled at the remark. He didn't see what Aisha seen in him. He was dark skin had thick eyebrows, which almost connected and was an inch shorter than her. Taron figured by her being a cheerleader, a 9th grader, and pretty that she wouldn't be interested in him.

"Stop playing, Aisha."

"I'm not playing." Aisha placed her phone back in the bag and crossed her arms. She really liked Taron. "Why would I be coming down here every day to see you after school then? My locker is on the third floor." She pointed to the ceiling.

"Aight... Call me later on."

"I'm going to call after practice."

Aisha gave Taron a peck on the cheek then headed towards the stairway that lead to the main entrance. She glanced back and caught Taron staring at her. "Stop looking at my fatty boy." She yelled down the hall. Taron smiled and turned to walk. He tensed up, while heading through the doors. Kids were coming and going from all floors. Taron moved slowly through the crowd then proceeded through the exit door. A lot of time had passed when he was talking to Aisha. He couldn't figure out which way to take home. The buses started to take off from the curb, but one lagged back and had the door open. A girl was climbing the steps as Taron strolled past.

"You getting on or not?" The bus driver asked.

Taron wanted to, but declined. He shook his head no. Taron wasn't familiar with all the stops yet. He didn't want to get on the bus and get dropped off in one of the crazy neighborhoods. Where, he was helpless and outnumbered. The driver closed the door then yanked away from the curb.

The two-lane street was backed up with traffic. Cars, trucks and teenagers riding pass the school trying to pick up friends and talk to girls made 9th Street come to a complete stand still at times. The teenagers were lawless. They didn't care who had somewhere to go. This was their time to shine in front of their peers. Crowds of students strolled on both sides viewing the daily scene. Some headed in the direction of the east side of Chester and others walked towards Kerlin Street. It remained the same though. They stayed on 9th Street until reaching their neighborhood or somebody picked them up riding down the street.

Taron didn't have any friends who owned a car or drove; he was 14 years old which was the age most boys and girls in Chester started selling and doing drugs, then having unprotected sex. He didn't chose to do either, not by force, but by choice. He wanted to be a regular kid and didn't want to end up like his brothers, Rashid and Malcolm. They stayed in and out of prison. Which he seen stress his mother out daily. Taron had made his mind up the day when Rashid was found not guilty for murdering a 19-year-old boy. On the way home from the courthouse, Taron's mother cried to Rashid and begged him to leave Chester and crime alone; period. Rashid had promised her that he would but lied. He was shot two weeks later coming out of her house. Taron had seen the bullet-ridden body and the pain in his mother's tears that day of his brother's murder. Taron promised her he would live a different life than them and, so far, that's what he was doing.

Taron decided to walk with the crowd of people straight down

9th Street to get home. The street was long and went through the whole city and was the main street that everybody traveled to get to their designations, within the city. He tried blending in with the others and it worked. The only thing that separated the kids was their jackets. Some had them on, while others decided not to. Taron was just passing the A-Plus Mini-Market when he spotted Tom-Tom and his followers standing in front of the Chinese store. They hadn't seen him yet, but were eyeing both sides of the street. Taron hesitated for a second and thought about running through the car lot, then taking the back way to the Bennett Homes. He turned in that direction, but stopped in mid-stride. Nobody paid attention to his sudden pause. The other boys and girls walked around him and continued with their conversations. Apple smiled at Taron. He was Tom-Tom's partner in crime. He had been the one who smacked Taron in the back of his head with the gum. Apple leaned up against a parked car talking to a young girl. He was a light skin youngster, with a demeanor that imitated the rapper TI and wore a black hooded sweatshirt, jeans and Timberland boots.

Apple was suspended from school for a month after him and the boys from the Highland Gardens got into a fight with the kids from the William Penn Projects. He was locked up that day and was caught with a knife. Apple didn't bother to move. He kept talking to the girl, but watched Taron. Apple rose up off the car and looked over to Tom-Tom and them to see, if anybody seen Taron walking by himself. They didn't though. Their attention was on the teenage boys leaping out of the cars across the street from the them.

After waiting for everybody to arrive and get out of their cars the project boys were ready for a brawl. Tom-Tom and them had got the best of them last time before the police came and broke it up.

Taron saw the incident about to unfold. Instead of running, today he would stay and watch the fight; at least until the cops arrived and broke it up. He would be safe then because everybody would be trying to get away and the cops wouldn't leave the surrounding areas until all the streets were cleared.

Apple stepped away from the girl without saying goodbye. The kids started forming a circle and cutting off traffic from both sides of the street. Apple was a block away. He could still see Tom-Tom leaning against the wall and fifteen project boys starting to walk over to them. Apple started running towards Taron. He wanted to black his eye first, then go help Tom-

Tom. Apple hated Taron. Taron knew it, but couldn't understand for what. He never did anything for Apple or Tom-Tom to have so much hatred against him.

Tom-Tom with his boys behind him met the project boys in the middle of 9th Street. Tom-Tom had a hand stuck inside of his black hoodie pocket like he had a weapon.

Apple raced down the street to be by Tom-Tom's side. He made it through the crowd by pushing, shoving and hitting innocence kids in order to stand next to Tom-Tom. Apple made it and stood on the front line with him.

Taron stood there in a daze waiting for the first blow to be thrown. He had silently hoped for Tom-Tom and Apple to get what they deserved for all of their times of picking on the weak, lonely and defenseless boys who didn't have the courage to fight back; including himself.

"Beep! Beep! Beep!" the sound of the horn blowing shook Taron out of his daze. He glanced over at the traffic and seen a blue four-door sedan with tinted windows. The window slowly came down. Malcolm stuck his head out of the window and yelled, "Get over here!"

Taron was reluctant, but he knew Malcolm would jump out of the car and body beat him in front of everybody. That's what big brothers did when you failed to obey them. Taron would feel more humiliated than he did now. Therefore, he hurried over to the car and got in on the passenger side. Malcolm was dressed casual. He wore a pair of denim jeans and navy blue Polo zip up hoodie. Taron placed his bag on floor then leaned back in the seat.

"What I tell you about being nosey and running to fights?" Malcolm said before pulling off with traffic heading in the opposite direction.

"I wasn't being nosey."

"Yes, you were and why you looking all scared?"

"I ain't scared of nothing." He lied to Malcolm. Taron could never tell Malcolm that he was scared from the fact that he was on the verge of being chased home today. Malcolm wouldn't go for it. He would make Taron fight all of them.

"Look, Taron I told you stop acting all timid and stuff...You can't be acting all weak around these buls."

"I'm not weak!"

"Yes, you are punk." Malcolm says, then punched Taron in the chest. "Stop being a punk or I'm going to pay some young buls to punish you every day until I break you out of that stuff."

"Ah... Stop hitting me like that," he said as he rubbed over his chest where Malcolm punched him.

"Look at you. Sounding like a little girl. That comes from you sitting in the house all day playing video games and mommy babying you." Malcolm stung him again, but on his arm. "You don't even hit back... I'm going to keep doing it until you start swinging back." He punched Taron in the stomach.

"Ah!" Taron bent over in pain, but didn't swing back.

André "Dre" Cooper

CHAPTER 3

The night enveloped the gloomy city and the temperature dropped to 33 degrees. It was normal for the October nights to get that cold. Which pushed many individuals into their homes.

In the living room, Cory and Taron sat on crates in the middle of the floor playing the video game, Call of Duty. They both stayed in the Bennett Homes Housing Project and lived a few doors away from each other. Taron had lived in the housing development all of his young life. Cory had been staying there for a little less than two years. He had been bouncing house-to-house with different relatives. Cory didn't like living there and constantly told his Aunt Bobbie. She tried to make it as comfortable as possible. He still didn't feel comfortable and felt lonely, and was depressed all the time. It didn't have anything to do with his environment. The issue was a little deeper than most knew.

At 6 years old, Cory lost both of his parents. They were killed a month apart. Cory's father, James, was murdered first. He had been a United States Marine, who had been deployed to Afghanistan. A month left to return home James was killed by a roadside bomb, while riding back to the base. The news devastated Chrissy. Cory's mother also served her country and was a registered nurse with the Army. Chrissy had been stationed in Iraq at the time of his death. They both were serving 18-month tours. On the news of his death, Chrissy became depressed and suicidal. A few days later, she committed suicide by swallowing a bottle of painkillers. James and Chrissy had been together since their teenage years. They battled all of life's difficulties, as well as Chester's poverty. Cory was their only child and they cherished him. However, he didn't think so. He felt that, if Chrissy loved him so much, why would she commit suicide and leave him to be alone. Cory didn't blame his father for nothing. He just grew a hatred for religion, but Cory kept these feelings to himself. Not even Taron knew about them, but Uncle Biz did. Trying to deal with all the pain and suffering of his parent's death drove Cory to become anti-social and depressed. He didn't like hanging around other kids, who had families or being around trouble making kids.

Despite all of his loses Cory still tried to be a normal kid. Nevertheless, this wasn't by chance. Uncle Biz had been breaking those layers of hatred down he had hidden away. Biz had been working on Cory for years now. It had been a hard and long road to get where he was at with Cory, but despite the circumstances, Biz felt Cory deserved at least a chance to make something of himself in life.

Biz had been in prison 22 years straight. Way before Cory was born. He was Chrissy's older brother who was imprisoned for murdering a man and received a life sentence for it. Cory adored his Uncle Biz and didn't question anything he said. He felt Biz was the only person that understood him and at least could relate to what he was going through, as a kid without parents. For the simple reason, Biz's father was murdered when he was young. By this fact, Biz knew exactly how to relate to his nephew. They had built a solid relationship through letters, visits and phone calls. The two talked at least twice a week. Biz had guided Cory through some rough times. He was the one who explained to Cory about life and being a good kid and staying out of trouble. He drilled it in Cory's head that prison wasn't the cool place that kids thought it was. And, that if he wronged or harmed people than that is where he would end up. Cory soaked all of the information up and tried to be more of a social kid, but at times he just couldn't. He was depressed. At the end of the day he missed his parents. That was the only thing Biz couldn't explain to Cory. Why God had chosen them? He knew the answer. Biz was a religious person, but Cory still didn't or wouldn't accept the answers.

"Why you leave me today?" Taron paused the game and stared at Cory.

"Man, I told you to meet me at the spot on time... I can't be waiting around all day. I thought you went the other way."

"You know I didn't leave the other way... We can't be walking in the main hallway without a pass."

"Well, tomorrow is football practice and we can lay back then just walk to practice after the streets clear up." Cory said, with a smile on his face. He loved the game. Cory had been playing since the age of five. Over the objections of Chrissy, James had signed Cory up to play in the city's football league. The Chester Panthers had a Peewee team and welcomed all of Chester's kids, who wanted to play. The staff felt that, if you caught a kid young and gave them a purpose in life or goal to reach that they would be productive kids, who wanted to live

26

and be someone in life.

"I might stop playing ball."

"Why?" Cory was confused. The two had met on the field and became best friends.

"I don't know. I just don't feel like playing no more."

"We going to be playing some good teams this year. You never know what schools might be watching us."

"Man, ain't no schools coming to Chester to see us."

"How you know? They came to see Kevin Jones."

"He played in Chi-Chester, not in the city."

"So what? We can make them come to see us by going hard. Just like Biz keep telling us."

"Ya uncle don't know what he talk'n about."

"Yes, he do!"

"Hey, cut all that arguing and loud noise up before I make ya'll put that damn game up." Aunt Boobie yelled from the top of the steps then went back into her room.

The two always got into little debates or arguments about everything. It never came to any blows being thrown, but they always challenged each other.

"I'm done playing this stupid game. We can't even talk in ya house." Taron placed the controller on the ground. "You trying to walk to the store?"

"Nah, I don't have any money. Aunt Boobie didn't get paid yet."

Taron got up and headed over to the sofa. He flopped down, then laid his head back. Cory followed him. This was their normal routine if they weren't practicing or playing video games for hours straight. Biz had suggested to them plenty of times that they should try to create their own game. When the ideal was first mentioned they loved it, but nobody put any effort into it. Biz had went so far and sent them a book on how write one. It had been sitting for months under Cory's bed. He never opened the book. Cory never told Biz that. Biz had thought that they took his advice and was working on it, but they weren't.

"I know how we can get some money."

"How?" Cory didn't believe him.

"Remember what Uncle Biz said about that video game stuff?"

"Man that stuff to hard."

"You never even tried to do it."

"So what..."

"Where the book he sent us?"

"Upstairs... That book got to many pages in it... I'm not trying to read all that."

"I don't either, but we got to find a way to make some money. You trying to sell some weed?"

Cory didn't bother to answer the question. Taron already knew the answer. They wanted to be different from other kids growing up in Chester and, or other urban communities.

"No... I'm going to be a football player."

"Me either, but I want to start dressing a little flyer. We at the

High now and all them girls going to be trying to holla at us. We going to need some money to at least chill with them."

"Yeah, I know."

"Let's just come up with some ideals first, then take turns reading the book."

Cory had agreed, so they sat back and started to think about all the hot games that they loved to play. It was a long list, but there favorites were the sport games and the shooting ones. Taron got up and started pacing the small living room. Aunt Boobie didn't have much in the house. A nice size television sat inside a wooden entertainment set. A three-piece sofa set and a couple wooden tables to hold the lamps on. She kept food in the house. Clothes on Cory's back and made sure he had everything that was needed. However, not all the extra luxurious things that were in a two parent home.

Aunt Boobie was James's younger sister. They had a small family; she had no kids and worked part-time at Harrah's Hotel and Casino. Which, she barely got by on.

Taron plopped back down on the sofa. "How about we make one about bullies?"

Cory thought for a minute then says, "what, we going to make a game about everybody chasing them around, who have been bullied then football tackling them one-by-one."

"Nah..."

"What then?'.'. Cory, asked.

"I don't know."

"We should make one about football."

"We can't make one like Madden dummy."

Taron was right, Cory thought. They needed to come up with a new kind of game. Cory laid his head back and closed his eyes. This routine had always worked for him to think about things or to just shut the whole world out. When every Cory was feeling neglected or lonely, he would go to his little world. He didn't want to tell Taron about it. Nor did Cory ever tell Biz. For one he thought, they would think that he was losing his mind and two; the world belonged to him only. He had fun there and didn't want anybody else to take part in it. Kids had the ability to do such things. Especially when trying to escape depression, abandonment, abuse and loneliness.

Cory drifted off. The place was called Firdous. He didn't know what the word meant or what it even described. Cory had heard it from one of his friends there one day. The place had a long spring that tasted of honey, but was clearer than water. The banks of the spring had tents of hollow pearls and all types of fruits you could think of grew around the spring's bank and off trees that occupied the whole place. Pretty boys and girls of all ages and colors roamed freely, but the teenage girls sat peaceful on thrones made of clouds. They wore green robes with gold trimmings and upon anybody arriving there, you had a choice of picking any friends you wanted. But, the one you picked would remain your companion the whole time there. If, it were a girl, she would do everything with you. From swimming in the pool of honey, helping you prepare the meals for the families to cheering for the boys and girls playing games. Cory felt loved at this place. They were free to do as they wanted with no adults supervising them nor was there any bullies allowed. Everybody was friendly and acted as normal kids should. They didn't need money to have fun nor did they worry about being bullied.

Upon arriving, Cory was dressed in a green robe. He began walking barefooted through the forest path. The place didn't resemble anything on earth. It was magical. A very fair girl with wild lovely eyes and intense black irises and long black hair stood up from her throne. The teenage girls had thrones arranged in ranks going across the sky. She waved Cory up to her. She wasn't the usual friend Cory came to visit. The other girl was a little darker and shorter, but just as pretty and innocence. He stopped. Hadiyah glided down and helped Cory up upon her throne.

"Where's Najibah?" Cory asked.

"She's around."

"Can I see her today?"

"No, you have work to do?.."

"Work! What kind of work?"

"Very important things to do... You don't know it now, but you are going to be a great benefit to society."

"A great benefit..."

"Yes."

"For what?"

"Don't worry you'll understand what I'm talking about later and ya'll remember this day I told you.".

"Well, what's your name?"

"Hadiyah."

Cory smiled at the beautiful name and how soft spoken the teenage girl was. "Could I ask you an question?"

"Yes."

"Could I stay here forever with you?"

Hadiyah blushed and it seemed like she glowed a little bit from the radiant smile that appeared on her face. This was their first encounter with each other. Cory had a pure soul that didn't contain any malice in it, and Hadiyah loved it.

"Not right now."

Taron shook Cory awake. He had been in a dream like state for the past ten minutes. Cory jumped a little and stared at Taron.

"What you do that for?"

"Man, you was sleep talking to ya self."

"Yo, don't wake me up when I'm sleep. You should've just went home or played the game until I woke up."

"You suppose to be thinking of a game ideal."

"I told you I got one."

"What?"

"The game where we get back at the bullies."

"It should be a shooting game."

"Yeah, people could get their frustration out on them like that."

"We could make it like... Where, you can download their faces to the game and we chase them around until we kill them all."

"I don't know about killing them." Cory said, with a crazy look on his face.

"Why not... Call of Duty got people getting killed and Grand Theft Auto... Kids still play them."

"Yeah, all them horror games got it to."

They stopped to think for a minute. Cory knew that they

needed more than just bullies being chased, but didn't want to put the killing in it. He never wanted to send people the message that killing was good. At least that's what Uncle Biz always told him. So what if the horror games condoned it. Cory wanted to be different from them.

"It's getting late. My mom is going to be calling my phone soon. I'm going to keep thinking about it tonight."

"Me too."

The two dapped each other hands then Taron headed for the door. Cory got off the sofa and sat back down on the crate. He picked the controller up and started playing the game.

CHAPTER 4

After Taron had left, Cory still failed to come up with any ideals on what type of video game to write.

It was late when Cory went upstairs to his room. Aunt Boobie had falling asleep before Taron had left. She needed some rest because of a few important appointments in the morning. For the past six months, Aunt Bobbie had been filling applications out for a new job. Better than the one she had. Her current one didn't pay much. Plus, it was only part-time employment. She figured that it was necessary to find a good steady income. After taking on the responsibility of raising Cory, she at least wanted him to have a good upbringing and not want for anything. Two companies had called her and wanted to see, if she was willing to come in for an interview. The first one she would be going to visit was for a paralegal position at a mid-size law firm. The job description didn't call for a college degree, although one would have helped, but they were looking for a reliable person that was computer savvy, could organize files and willing to learn on the go. Aunt Boobie fit the criteria perfect. She didn't go to college, but did graduate from a trade school that dealt with computer programming. The other interview was for a clerical position at Crozer Medical Center. Either one of the jobs would provide her with a nice salary along with benefits.

Cory laid under the covers with his eyes wide open. He had been tossing and turning all night. For some reason he couldn't sleep. He kept thinking about football, his parents, school and those kids who kept bulling him. Cory was tired of running. Every day seemed like a huge challenge. Cory knew that he could beat them, at least one-on-one. He just was scared of the repercussions. Whether, he would end up shot or even worst killed. The boys were known troublemakers and had access to all types of weapons. This fact was well-known. They came from the Highland Gardens and hung around nothing but thugs. Cory thought about telling his Uncle Biz and then decided not to. He didn't want Uncle Biz to think that he was soft or incapable of defending himself. Cory felt that he needed to figure this problem out by himself because he didn't have anybody else to turn to. After coming to the conclusion that he didn't know how to handle the problem Cory mind drifted back to football and video games. They would be hitting tomorrow at practice, in order to be ready for the game of the season. It would be huge for him, personally. College recruiters would attend.

Cory had done well in all the games so far. He played the corner-back position. Cory averaged two interceptions and one touchdown a game. So this reason alone made him excited about practicing. Cory loved the game and felt that it was going to be his ticket out of Chester. He couldn't wait to make it to the NFL and leave all of his troubles behind. This was one of the motivating factors that pushed Cory to be a good person and strive hard at the game.

A light vibrating sound was coming from his desk drawer. Cory peeked over top of the covers. The light on his phone was blinking every time it vibrated. He threw the covers off of him and stepped out of the bed. Cory had on a pair of boxers and t-shirt with no socks on. The room was small and didn't have much inside except a twin-sized bed, nightstand and small television. There were no pictures hanging up or sitting on any stands of his family. The room was bare. All he used it for was sleep. Cory glanced at the caller ID and shook his head. It was Taron calling. Cory grabbed the phone then turned it off. He wasn't trying to rap so late at night. Cory thought before getting back in the bed then throwing the covers over his head. The phone had messed his train of thought up. He sat there for a moment trying to figure out what he was just thinking about. "Oh!" Cory thought. "The video game!" Coming up with the ideal was harder than he thought. He knew how to play the games. What games everybody played and liked. But all of those games were already made. Cory put his hands behind his head and closed his eyes. He quickly fell asleep.

* * * * *

The room had a slight airy feeling. It was pitch dark inside and all that could be heard was Taron's low voice. He laid across the bed in a pair of shorts and t-shirt. Taron had the phone glued to his ear and eyes closed.

"I'm coming to ya practice tomorrow." Aisha said. She was getting more determined and aggressive with Taron. Aisha really had a thing for the eighth grader. His grade didn't matter to her though, because they both were the same age. Aisha had just started school early, but she never told Taron yet.

"How you going to come when you got practice too?"

"It's some type of meeting tomorrow, so we're not going to have it after school. Why you don't want me to come? You better not have another girl going to ya practices because I'm not even with that."

"What I tell you about that?"

"What?" She started blushing. Aisha knew exactly what he was talking about.

"You my girl now."

"I better be or I'm going to be whipping somebody tomorrow at that field."

"Girl, you can't fight."

"Yeah okay... Try me than... Go ahead and tell her to come and you'll see that I'm 'bout that life!'" She busted out laughing.

The two had been going on like this for hours. It was their first conversation on the phone and they had already committed to each other.

Aisha had all the lights out in her room. She laid under the covers, in a fetal position, whispering to Taron. It was way past her bedtime. Normally, she would be getting her beauty sleep, but wasn't and insisted, that Taron stay on the phone. Aisha wanted to savor the moment of talking to her future husband, as she told him; those being her very words to Taron. He responded only with a simple laugh like it was a joke. Taron couldn't understand how she fell for him so quick. Aisha had failed to tell him that, he was her very first childhood crush and boyfriend.

She lived with both parents in a neighborhood called Nova Scotia. It was located on the east side of Chester, but only well-to-do families lived there. Having a two-parent household was unusual in Chester, though there were some, but for the most part the kids either lived with their mother or father or some relatives of the family took care of them. Aisha's parents were involved with every aspect of her life. They had guarded her, so far from the harsh conditions of Chester, but they knew someday that she would become aware of it. Aisha understood the conditions though. She knew to stay away from drugs, gang violence and all the other negative things that could bring a kid down. That's why Aisha was so into Taron. He was different she thought. Aisha had been watching him closely. He didn't hang with the drug dealers, didn't do drugs, had a nice personality and was handsome. She figured that her parents wouldn't object to Taron being her friend.

"Bring ya friend with you, too."

"I am... My girl don't go anywhere without me... That's my best friend."

"Where's she from?"

"She's from Toby Farms. I'm going to be spending the weekend at her house. Ya'll going to come up there?"

"I don't know. We don't have a car or nothing."

"Boy, I know. Ya'll could walk up there or catch the bus or something."

"I don't know. I'll see what's up with Cory first. I might be able to get my brother to drop us off."

"Well, you better see what you can do because I want to see you over the weekend."

"Won't ya'll just come to our game on Saturday. We play down Memorial Park."

43

"I got to ask Renee. She should be with it. Renee trying to holla at ya bul anyway... Hold up for a second." Aisha moved the phone from her ear. She had heard some footsteps like they were heading to her room. "Taron, my dad just came in from work and he always comes into check on me before he goes to bed... I'm going to call you back... Aight?"

"Aight."

"I love you!" She whispered.

Taron hesitated then says, "Me too."

* * * * *

Cory was stretched out across the clouded floor. Hadiyah sat with her legs crossed watching him. She touched Cory lightly on his shoulder. He awoke and smiled at the charming girl. Cory sat there for a moment, then rolled over to sit up.

"You must be worried about something." Hadiyah said.

"I was thinking about you."

"For what? You're unable to be with me. There's a lot of requirements and obligations in order for you to be with me."

44

"What if I had money and got on my hands and knees and begged you to leave with me?" asked Cory.

"Money doesn't mean anything to me... Look around... We have everything... And, you wouldn't have to beg to be with me. I would love to be your companion... It's just not that simple."

"Then why do I keep coming back here than?"

Hadiyah didn't answer the question. She stood up and glanced over the throne's terrace. Hadiyah scanned below the area of her domain. She made a few movements with her hands and lowered the palace. Hadiyah stepped off the clouded throne followed by Cory.

The two strolled hand-and-hand through the forest. They were quiet and occasionally smiled at each other. Cory couldn't understand her remarks from his questions. The constant visits to the place had Cory puzzled. Why was he constantly showing up there, if he couldn't stay or bring Hadiyah with him?

They came upon a river that had diamond-like rocks along the banks. All types of colorful fish swam inside of it, in one direction. An odd looking fish stood up over top of the water.

Hadiyah seen it first, then shrugged Cory and pointed towards the river.

"What is that?"

"It's a sign. We must follow it." She pulled Cory along to get a closer glimpse of the fish. Upon them getting a closer view the fish dropped back in the river and started moving slowly upstream, in the opposite direction of the other fishes. Hadiyah and Cory closely followed. A few yards upstream, the fish came to a stop. Hadiyah was the first to raise her head. A velvet-like green carpet spread across the ground, and a man with his whole body covered in white soft linen with gold trim around the seams sat on the carpet. His face couldn't be seen, but his eyes remained uncovered and alert. Hadiyah stopped upon seeing the man. She whispered to Cory. "This is what the fish was leading us to."

"Who's that?"

"He's one of the wise men."

"Wise men? I got a question for him."

Hadiyah pulled Cory along by his hand. She mumbled

something under her breath, then stopped at the top of his carpet. The man raised his head.

"I am Hadiyah."

"Hadiyah the daughter of Nabilah?"

"Yes."

"And, this is Cory, the son of James."

"Yes," stuttered Cory.

"My friend has come to ask you for some guidance. He's confused, orphaned and depressed. Please benefit him with any knowledge that you can."

The man waved for the couple to take a seat on the carpet.

They followed his invitation and sat down. Cory was curious of the man. How did he know his name, and his father's? "What is your name?"

"My name is Sage."

"I have a problem that I don't know how to solve."

Sage stared at Cory's gentle eyes. He was a kid lost. Sage could see the hurt, confusion and loneliness. He rested both hands on his knees. Sage had a light skin complexion and appeared to be a regular size man. His voice betrayed youth, but Sage's eyes showed intelligence.

"You have a number of problems that need to be resolved."

"Yes."

"You have not yet reached the peak of your journey. Remain patience. The hardships you are facing now are only temporary. They will surely past and you will be granted much success, if you remain true to your nature. Be thankful of the things you have, dutiful to your family and be a good friend to your neighbor. One more thing, the recompense for an evil is an evil like thereof; but whoever forgives and make reconciliation, his reward will be something that he can't even imagine... Abundant."

"What about Hadiyah? I want to be with her." Cory pleaded to Sage. He turned and glanced at Hadiyah. She dropped her head down. Hadiyah understood it was impossible for Cory to be with her, but she knew Sage wouldn't harm Cory with such information.

"I only tell you of the things that I know."

Hadiyah grabbed Cory by the hand and then stood up. Sage was finished with them. He had already answered Cory's questions. Those words of wisdom would take Cory far, if he applied them properly with the right intentions.

André "Dre" Cooper

CHAPTER 5

The day had been uneventful. Cory and Taron made it to school on time without any problems from the bullies. During, the eighth graders lunch period Aisha and Renee had stayed back. They sat and ate lunch with Cory and Taron. The other boys and girls were eyeing them. They had gained some cool points or popularity by the girls doing that. None of the other boys were dating any ninth graders and only a few girls had boyfriends in a higher grade. Cory and Renee also had got along well with each other. She thought he was good-looking, and that she had to be his girl. The boys were new to the school and soon all the rest of the girls would be trying to get their attention. They wouldn't be eighth graders forever. Next year they would be moving around on the upper floors where some girls would be trying to throw themselves at them. Especially with the boys being into sports.

Last period came, Cory and Taron didn't rush out as usual. They had stayed back with Aisha and Renee. The girls were going to walk home with them, then go to their practice from there. Taron had come up with an excuse to stay after-school for a half-hour. He lied and told them that he had to stay back for a while in order to talk with a teacher. Cory knew it was bogus. He didn't want the girls to see how the other boys would treat them, if they were spotted walking home. After seeing them fail to fight back and getting beat on, Taron didn't know how the girls would react. He might lose his girlfriend or better yet receive a broken jaw or something. Taron wasn't willing to take that chance, either way, so lying was the best thing to do. At least that's what Taron thought. Cory didn't agree or mind that Taron had lied. He didn't want to face them with the girls either. Taron faked it and went to talk to his teacher, while Cory and the girls were waiting at his locker talking. He finished then they all left school and took the back way to the Bennett Homes. The girls wanted to walk down 9th Street, but they agreed with the boys that the back way would be quicker. Their football practice started at five o'clock and they had to walk there too.

The group stopped at Cory's house. Aunt Bobbie wasn't home

yet. Aisha and Renee stayed, while Taron ran home to get dressed. Cory ran upstairs to his room. He started taking all of his clothes off. Renee snuck up to his room. Cory was pulling up his padded pants when he noticed Renee standing in the doorway. She just stared. Renee had on her pleaded skirt and yellow shirt. Cory's shirt was off. Little stomach muscles poked out of his youthful body.

"Uh..." Renee said, at the site of his chest.

"Yeah, I know."

"You know what?"

"You like what you see."

"Maybe." Renee stepped in the room and sat on the bed. Cory went over to her, and sat beside her.

"What'd you come up here for?"

"I wanted to see what ya room looked like."

"That's all?"

"Yup! Why what you thought I came up here for?" She said and leaned into kiss Cory on the lips.

"What ya'll doing?" Aisha asked walking into his room.

"Nothing," Renee explained, then got up off the bed and walked over to Aisha's side. Renee was embarrassed by Aisha catching her trying to give Cory a kiss. She didn't want Aisha to think she was fast. "I was just caught in the moment," Renee said, to herself and would tell Aisha that same excuse later on.

Cory didn't bother to say anything to Aisha. He was upset she had just walked into his room unannounced. Nobody evaded his privacy. Even, Aunt Bobbie knocked before she entered his room. He started putting on his shirt then headed over to the closet for some other things. Cory grabbed his bag with all of his essential items in it except for his pads and helmet.

"Renee, could you hold my bag for me while I carry these pads and stuff?"

Renee lit up. She was happy to do anything for Cory. "Yeah, give it here." Renee walked over and he handed it to her before heading out of the room. The girls followed his lead.

Taron was stepping in the door as they were coming down the steps. He stared at everybody with a curious grin. "Ya'll ready?"

"We good." Cory answered.

"Let me hold ya bag, boo." Taron handed Aisha his bag, while he carried the helmet and pads.

Taron stepped out of the house followed by the rest them. He walked wondering why everybody was upstairs. Did Cory try Renee? He didn't think so, because Cory was the shy type. Cory would never make the first move. Plus, they had just met. Was Renee one of those fast girls? It was possible, but he didn't know. Taron never heard anything bad about her. And, he didn't think Aisha would be around any girls like that.

The weather had been nice and warm throughout the day, so they took the back way to the Memorial Park. The group wanted to savor the weather and moment. Taron and Aisha walked a few feet ahead of Cory and Renee. Aisha was holding his hands and laughing at all of his silly jokes. The two were becoming comfortable around each other. This lead them to letting their guards down and being cool to talk about anything. They were building a true bond. The group got to the park five minutes before practice.

The grass shined in the sun's autumn glow. At the entrance of the park a nice sized football field spread out. The field was

100 yards. Several hills decorated both ends of the goals and on the left side of the field. Trees, brush and a flat plain made up the players sideline. Memorial Park had been the Chester Panthers practice and home field since the league begun. The park was located on Chester's west side. It sat on the side of 9th Street and was separated from the Highland Gardens neighborhood by an old hospital called, Sacred Heart Medical Center.

Aisha and Renee stood on the sidelines, as all the boys were lined up in six rows with 8 boys in each of them. Taron and Cory suited up then filled in the back rows. It was a small crowd of parents and friends watching the boys practice for the day. Some sat in lawn chairs on the sidelines, while others stood on the hills taking in the full view.

Night started falling quickly and practice was coming to an end. The boys had been going hard for two hours straight. The weather began to drop and the girls started filling the chill. Their tiny skirts and sweat shirts, that Cory and Taron had packed for them, were providing no relief.

Taron lined up behind the quarterback. He played the running back position on offense and occasionally was a defensive end when he was needed for defense. The offense was trying a new play. They had been practicing it all day and the coach wanted to know, if the defense could stop it.

Cory stood in the corner back position. He had been born strictly to play this defensive position. No kids his age or a little older performed it better. The coaches knew it, as well as the rest of kids in the league. Cory was destined to play on the Division 1 level, if he kept his nose clean and continued working on his game throughout the years. The sky would be the limit for him. He crouched over, slightly. He was trying to read the offense. The offensive formation and the play that was being called out was new to him. He had never seen it.

"Left 23! Left 23!" The quarterback barked out looking at the receiver on the left side. He stood up and seen the defense were ready to blitz. The quarterback couldn't get the new play off. He pointed at Cory and made the offense aware of the play.

"Left! Left! Hut! Hut!" He had made an audible.

Cory came racing at the offensive line. The quarterback faked a pass to the left. Which froze most of the secondary, then turned to the right and threw a shuttle pass to Taron. He caught it. The whole right side of the field was wide open and the goal was in full view.

After the fake Cory backed peddled then turned around and ran full speed to the right side. He was two feet behind Taron running up the sideline. Taron was fast, but Cory was determined.

He hulked Taron down on the 3-yard line and dove at him. They fell down, but as Taron was falling, he stretched out trying to score the goal.

This was the boys element. All of the their aggression and determination were incorporated when they played. Once Cory and Taron got on that field, they had no fear. They were the ones planting the seeds of fear in their opponent's hearts.

Aisha and Renee just watched in amazement at how the two friends were so good and focused on the sport. The whole practice Cory or Taron didn't bother to even glance over at the girls. They didn't acknowledge them. It wasn't about Aisha and Renee. Cory and Taron had a goal. They wanted to be NFL players. Their coaches and a few other people that wanted them to succeed had drilled into their heads that, playing at the highest level wasn't going to come easy. So they wanted to be good every time they stepped foot on the field, and they did just that.

The coach singled that Taron had scored the touchdown. He did it by going the extra mile to stretch out when he was getting tackled. Cory was heated. You could see it all in his demeanor when getting up after the play. The offensive players ran up the field and congratulated Taron on the effort.

Taron leaped up off the ground. He raced over to catch Cory walking to the bench and smacked Cory on the butt and kept running while laughing. Taron had got him today, but he knew Cory would get revenge. Cory made it over to the bench. He started gathering all of his things up and placing them in his bag. Taron stood by his side doing the same.

"I got you today."

"You got me... You ain't fast though."

"I smoked you down the side line."

"I had to run all the way back from the scrimmage line."

"What ever... You didn't catch me."

"I tackled you at the 1-yard line."

"I scored and that's all that counts."

The coaches, players and families were all clearing out of park. Cory waved the girls over, in order for them to walk back to the Bennett with them. It was getting dark and cold. They were going to walk straight down 9th Street. Aisha and Renee made it over to them. The group headed up the hills trying to make it to lit street.

"How ya'll going to get home?" Cory asked.

A group of boys strolled out of the side street. They seen Taron and Cory then stopped. Nobody had seen the small group of boys standing on the side of the car.

"We're going to catch the bus. Why? You got a way for us to get home?" Renee asked.

"Nah, I was just asking because it's getting late and ya'll haven't been home yet."

"We good."

The boys waited until they got a few feet ahead of them then ran out. Tom-Tom was in front and Apple was right by his side holding an arm's length tree trunk.

Aisha heard the steps first and turned around. "Watch out, ya'll!"

Everybody turned to see what was happening. At the site of Tom-Tom and Apple approaching, Taron's heart dropped. He wanted to run, but couldn't.

"Yeah, caught you suckers now," yelled Apple.

Everybody froze, while Tom-Tom and his eight boys surrounded the group. Cory was at a loss for words. His brain began racing on trying to figure a way out of the mess. Aisha glanced at Taron for help, but he wouldn't look at her so she turned her eyes on Cory.

"Come on Tom-Tom, why you starting trouble?" asked Renee.

"Ae Renee, what you doing around these buls? Ya brother know you all the way down here with these lames?"

"Yeah..." She lied. Renee was just trying to save them from getting jumped. She knew Tom-Tom well. He was cool with her brother, who also was a bully and prayed on the weak.

"Matter of fact! You and Aisha get outta here before ya'll get caught up in this." Apple yelled at the two.

Cory and Taron remained still. They looked at each other twice and contemplated running and leaving the girls. They couldn't though. Both were carrying too much equipment to run at their full speed and get away.

Without warning, Apple pushed Renee out of the way. He swung the tree trunk at Taron's arm.

"Ahh."

Apple landed the blow in the upper part of his arm. Taron dropped everything and covered his face. The boys swarmed on Taron and Cory. Tom-Tom punched Cory on the side of his head. He dropped to the ground and balled up. Apple landed another blow, but at Taron's thigh. He was trying to get Taron to drop his hands, so he could get a clear face shot. Taron dropped his hands, but fail on the ground.

"Stop! Stop! Stop!" Aisha and Renee yelled together. They tried grabbing some of the boys, but were getting pushed and knocked down.

They started stomping and kicking hard. Cory and Taron both were balled up in the fetal position trying to cover their faces and head. It wasn't working. They were getting nailed each times.

Aisha leaped up off the ground and started pushing the boys again. Cars and trucks were slow rolling down the street watching the fight. Renee ran in the middle of traffic. She was trying to get somebody to help, but they didn't. The woman stayed in her car and beeped the horn twice at Renee. She tried to run over to the window. The woman pulled off. This was common in Chester. Everybody was scared of the consequences of helping. So, instead of helping they minded their business and watched innocent kids get beat and stomped by mobs.

They stopped stomping them and started to walk off. Apple and Tom-Tom stared at the girls with a slight grin. It was funny to them.

Renee ran over to Cory. "You okay? You okay?" She was trying to help him up.

"Ah, hold up! Hold up!" Cory tried to get up, but was in pain.

Taron was slumped over bleeding from his nose. Aisha sat on the ground by his side. She tried helping him get up, but he shook his head no; he was in pain.

After sitting on the ground for five minutes, the girls helped the boys up. Cory and Taron just stared at each other. Words couldn't explain the pain and damage done to them. Their noses bled and both had black eyes, but the most damage had been to their pride and self-esteem. They had just got a beating because they wanted to be and were different from the rest of the kids.

The group walked to Taron's house in silence. Nobody said a word. Once at Taron's house, Malcolm was there and seen the work done to his brother's face, he was crushed; but remained calm. Malcolm then gave the girls a ride home where they explained the whole story to him.

CHAPTER 6

The October morning brought a light chill. As normal, the traffic was flowing and the long yellow school buses were carrying kids to their designated places. Cory and Taron walked to school, by going the normal route today. They headed straight down 9th Street. It was crowded with kids of all ages trying to make it to the different schools in the surrounding area.

After icing their wounds, the swelling had gone down over night and all that remained was the black eyes. Taron's stood out more because both of his were tinted. But, Cory's tattooed eye also was blackish red. Aunt Bobbie had begged Cory to stay home for the day, in order to let his eye and body heal. Cory refused to. His body wasn't hurting. The black eye was the only thing that remained of the bully's damage and a broken spirit, but other than that he was okay. The two had a long conversation when he came in banged up. Aunt Bobbie was concerned with his well-being. She wanted and needed to know, if these boys always picked on them or not. He denied it. Cory had made up a story about him being at the wrong place at the wrong time. She didn't believe it, but couldn't do nothing about it. Cory wouldn't open up to her. He knew she didn't believe the story and felt sad about having to lie. He hated lying. Cory just didn't want Aunt Bobbie worrying about him getting hurt every time he left the house. Cory was going to deal with it. He just couldn't figure out how to. He didn't want to go to the police, and he was scared of opening up to anybody; especially to the police and other family members. Would they believe him? Could they provide real protection or any at all? What if they didn't and he got labeled a snitch, then Cory would be placed in an even graver danger, at least that was the scenario he contemplated.

Cory turned to Taron. "You alright?"

"I'm aight." Taron responded without looking at him.

"Did Aisha call last night?"

"Yeah, I talked to her for a while... She understands what's going on with them."

"Renee does too... She said, her brother act just like them, but I don't have to worry about him now because he locked up." Cory chuckled a little.

"Tom-Tom and Apple need to be right with him..."

"Taron, I'm not going to the cops on them because they ain't going to do nothing, but talk to them then let them back on the streets."

"Me either... I was just saying that because they keep messing with us, because we not standing up for ourselves... I think that's what we need to do... Stand up for ourselves... It's only right."

"I know, but we can't beat all of them... How we going to stand up to them?"

Taron couldn't come up with an answer to the problem and didn't try to. He was just tired, depressed and desperate to end it all. At the moment, he thought about Malcolm. After dropping the girls off home, Malcolm went back to the house. Taron had been sitting on the sofa with his mother. She sat there crying and cursing the boys, who did it to him. She wanted to call the authorities. Taron wouldn't let her. Every time she reached for the phone, he grabbed it and hung it up. Taron tried to convince his mom that the police wouldn't help. The school wouldn't help and nobody else would either. There were no programs, in place, that prevented such crimes. This was the culture in Chester. The culture robbed the youth of their childhood and nobody was trying to reverse the fact. She knew and understood it. She was born and raised in Chester. It was a violent city, who citizens prayed on each other's weakness. Malcolm had stormed in the house. He wanted revenge. Malcolm promised his mom that he would stay out of it, but Malcolm lied as he always did to her. The boys had targeted his family. And, if left unchecked, they would do it again. Malcolm escorted Taron upstairs to his room, in order to talk in private. He sat in there for two hours scolding Taron. This time Taron didn't show any fear or weakness. He was upset, depressed, and tired of being took advantage of. He still wouldn't agree to what Malcolm was preaching. Taron was scared of prison. Just like any ordinary kid should or would be. It wasn't a pretty place for kids or anyone for that matter. And the actions Malcolm was trying to convince him to do would surely lead the 14 year old there.

"You going to be ready for that game this weekend?" Cory

asked.

"Of course! These black eyes ain't going to stop me from getting on that field." Taron says, as they were walking in front of the school. "Ae, let's walk through the side door. I'm not trying to be getting all stared at by the whole school."

"Aight."

They continued walking down the street. Cory reached in his backpack and grabbed two pair of sunglasses. "Huh?" Taron grabbed a pair and looked them over.

"These jawns is good." He placed them on his face. "And, they fit perfect."

Taron and Cory made it to the side door. At the time, no teachers were arriving or walking into the building. Just as they were about to leave, a teenage girl stepped out of the door.

"Hold it for us." Taron yelled. She held the door and they walked in. The staircase was packed with kids. Taron looked to the left and seen boys standing around talking. Cory stepped in and focused his eyes on the boys sitting on the steps to the right. His heart skipped a beat.

"Look at the two little girls sneaking into school through the back." Apple said, while sitting on the steps.

Tom-Tom sat beside Apple along with the same group of boys, who jumped them the night before. After Apple made the statement everybody, in the stairway, started laughing.

Taron glanced around the crowd. He reached under his jacket and pulled a loaded 9mm out of his waistline. Everybody stopped laughing and stared at the weapon, then scattered. The kids dispersed in every direction. Some ran out of the side door, while others ran to the hallway, but Tom-Tom and Apple stayed. They didn't fear the gun or death. Chester had made them numb to fear and death. They welcomed both with open arms.

"What you going to do with that?" Tom-Tom asked.

Taron started stepping towards them. Aisha and Renee were rounding the top of the steps when they were stopped in their tracks. Aisha and Renee stood behind Tom-Tom and Apple.

"Nooo!" Aisha screamed.

He stopped upon hearing Aisha's voice. Taron had been in a

trance every since pulling the weapon out. He had blocked everything and everybody out except the small group of boys sitting in front of him.

Cory leaped in front of Taron holding the gun. "No man, we can't do it like this... This not the way... Don't throw ya life away on these buls. Not like this!"

Taron was trying to look past Cory. He needed to keep his eye on them. Taron started moving the gun around trying to get a good shot at Apple.

Tom-Tom and Apple jumped up holding weapons of their own.

"What! What!" Apple yelled at Taron.

Cory turned around with his hands held in the air. He was stuck in the middle of a Mexican standoff. Cory didn't move or show any fear. He was trying to be extra careful in this situation. The side door burst opened and Ms. Benson came storming in.

"Oh my God! Please kids put the guns down... Please put the guns down."

Nobody turned to look at her.

"Tom-Tom it ain't worth it... We just tired of ya'll bullying us. That's all... We don't want no problems." Cory was upset it had come to this conclusion. They never were supposed to confront them with guns. Average kids didn't solve problems like that. They went about it the normal way of dealing with issues of getting bullied and sometimes people listened and helped out, and at times they didn't. Pulling a weapon on the bully would not solve the problem. Cory knew this and thought Taron did too.

Ms. Benson stepped next to Cory. She focused her eyes on Taron. She knew him well. Taron was a student in her class. "Please Taron, put the gun down, baby. You don't want to ruin your life like this. You have a future..." She turned and spoke to the rest of the boys. "All of you have futures. A family that loves you and by committing this act... Everybody loses... Everybody loses... Please, we're not all going to get along at times, but this is not the solution to the problem. This is not how ordinary people solve problems. Put the guns down and let's walk to my class and solve the issue. I'm sure we could. For every problem there's always a solution, but this is not the way."

"Apple, we just want to be left alone." Cory spoke.

"Well, why ya man pulling guns out than? You don't want to be left alone if ya'll running around here carrying guns."

"This... This, is the first time I ever seen him with a gun. I promise you this is not how we planned to do it... Like, we were willing to fight... Not shoot."

Tom-Tom and Apple wasn't backing down or buying Cory's plea.

Ms. Benson turned around facing Taron. He still had his gun aimed high. Tears started running down his cheeks. Taron didn't want to shoot anybody. He couldn't even figure out why he stole the gun out of Malcolm's bedroom last night. His depression drove him to do it, but his compassion for life was stopping Taron from pulling the trigger. All he wanted to do was be a regular kid, who enjoyed life and played football. He never asked to live in this hostile environment where you had to show aggression and strength, in order to survive. Only in Chester was that the motto. Taron couldn't conquer or face his fears this way. Pulling a gun out. No! That was a coward's way of trying to solve the problem. Not of a sane thinking person. He realized at that moment, no it wasn't Tom-Tom and Apple he was scared of. Taron was scared to challenge his mind and come up with a better solution than violence. Pulling guns out was too easy. That's why it was the first action he used when he got depressed, and was also why it was the first action done by most kids when the depression or problem was to deep to handle. By doing this, he was living and following the same principals, as the bullies, so at that very moment he decided to follow his own emotions and rules which was telling him to end it all.

Ms. Benson walked, slowly, over to Taron. He raised the gun to his head and yelled. "I'm tired of this! I can't take it no more! I can't take!"

Everybody just stared at Taron. They were shocked. The whole room froze. Nobody wanted to make a sudden move and trigger Taron in to pulling the trigger.

"No! We can talk this out... Please, no!" Cory said.

"Taron, you have a future sweetie. Please, let's talk this out first... Please, put the gun down... You have a family that loves you and cares... I love you! Cory loves you! We all love you! Please, don't do it..." Ms. Benson responded to Taron's threat.

Taron dropped the weapon on the ground and his head slumped

down. He wanted to do it but couldn't. Ms. Benson's words spoke to his soul. Taron couldn't cheat his family and friends this way. He had to face his problems head on and deal with them. Taron dropped to his knees.

Tom-Tom tapped Apple on the stomach. They both tucked their weapons away. Apple walked down the steps and headed out of the door with Tom-Tom and them in tow. They hadn't expected Taron to pull a gun out and even though he did it still didn't matter to them whether he took his own life or not. They were ready to deal with the problem, their way. The turn of events shocked them though. That along with Ms. Benson and Cory's words of hope. Nobody had spoken to them in such a manner. It made them second-guess some of the principals they held on to in life. All they knew how to do was to gain respect through violence and putting their foot on the timid ones necks, in order to get what they wanted.

Aisha and Renee stood at the top of the steps in tears. This was the closes ever to there being a school shooting. There wouldn't be any Columbine styled or Sandy Hook type of shooting in any of the schools in Chester. No! The kids that were depressed scared and felt like life was worthless would never come in school shooting at innocence bystanders. They couldn't do it. Their state mind was different. These kids would just continue to run from their problems and fears or commit suicide to end it all forever. This would be their method of dealing with stress and problems until they gained the courage to notify the proper people, who were in position to deal with these types of issues. They would never go to the extremes of pulling a gun out on anybody but themselves.

Taron was different and he was willing to show the boys how different he was. He didn't pull the trigger and never wanted to, but he wanted to take his own life not theirs. Taron felt that he couldn't handle the pressure, so ending it by killing himself would solve the problems. But he was wrong and realized it when Ms. Benson spoke.

CHAPTER 7

One Year Later

The sun stood directly above the swarms of people which made it feel a little hotter than it normally would've been on the September afternoon. A small breeze would past, occasionally, that brought some relief, but not much to the crowds. They didn't care though. They were willing to stand, shoulder-to-shoulder, and take the heats punishment for the day. It didn't matter. Everybody wanted to be a part of the historic event. Students, teachers, families and State Officials were in attendance. They were all there to show their support to the Break Free Foundation. The event was being sponsored by the City of Chester, in order to help push Break Free agenda and goals of stopping bullies and promoting their new app, which was going to be available in Apple's app store after the event.

A 4ft stage had been setup and stood in front of the goal line with the park's rolling hills to its back. The City had also placed 3 foot gates around the stage, in order to protect the music equipment and provide security to the public officials seated on the stage. Twenty metal seats were lined up on the stage with a pulpit standing in the center and microphone hooked to it. Memorial Park had been transformed into a pep rally type of atmosphere. Venders, banners with Break Free splashed across the bottom part of the stage, people with Break Free t-shirts and hats were spread throughout the park. Booths were setup that offered free food and games to the kids and adults were also scattered around the place.

Cory and Taron sat next to each other. They both wore white t-shirts with Break Free written in black and denim jeans along with white sneakers. Ms. Benson sat next to Taron with Aisha and Renee by her side. They were also groomed in Break Free t-shirts and jeans. The group was all smiles. This event had been a long time in the making and they were trying to soak in every moment of it. After the incident happened in school with Taron pulling the gun out on the bullies then turning the gun on himself, Ms. Benson had finally had enough.

She was tired of how the kids were being bullied, then neglected physically and mentally by their parents and others.

Nobody was trying to help or seemed to care. Everybody wanted to evade the problems by turning a blind-eye to the issues confronting the kids and adults alike. Ms. Benson wanted to help. A few weeks after the incident Ms. Benson sat down with the group to talk about the bullies and wanted them to express their feelings about them and to explain what they thought should be done about it. This discussion went on for some months before Cory and Taron came up with an ideal. They wanted to form a support group of students and citizens, who would volunteer to walk kids' home from school. They didn't want to limit the program to just high school students, but throughout the City of Chester. Any section of the City that had a school, Cory wanted Break Free members there to help provide a safe passage home for the kids. This included placing members on school buses and at bus stops. It took a while to gain some momentum, but the program took off. For the simple reason that, Cory got the Chester High basketball players to become one of Break Free's first group of members to join their cause. After students seen the team participate in the program everybody else started to follow. There was also the successful recruitment done by Ms. Benson when she gave a passionate speech to a large crowd of parents and students during the school's Home Coming event. She had come forward and admitted to being a victim of bullies. Ms. Benson had been getting picked on and harassed by strangers and friends on a few social network sites for a couple of years, at the time. She had drove the point home with the crowd that being a victim of bullies wasn't just limited to Chester or kids, but it had became a nationwide problem that touched many lives young and old, and it needed to be stopped.

Cory stood up and headed towards the pulpit. The crowd started cheering and screaming, "Break Free... Break Free..." Cory raised his hand, in order to quiet the audience then spoke. "I would like to thank ya'll for coming out here today and supporting this 'Break Free movement... And, we also would like to thank the City of Chester for closing all the schools today, in order for everybody to make it here for the event..." The kids went wild. "But, before we began I want to start the event off by presenting Break Free's newest member, who at one point in his life was a bully and bullied me... I forgave him and we at Break Free embraced him with opened arms."

The crowd cheered and clapped at Cory's opening statement. Taron smiled, as he pushed a teenage boy in wheelchair across the stage. The boy had a Break Free t-shirt on with denim jeans and white sneakers. He was dressed exactly like Taron and

Cory. Taron made it to the pulpit with the boy.

Cory grabbed the mic and unhooked it from the stand then gave it to the boy. Taron maneuvered the wheelchair around a little trying to find a good place for him to view the crowd and speak. The boy accepted the mic then spoke, "How's everybody doing today?"

"Good!" the crowd yelled.

"Well, my name is Apple... Some of you may know me and others might not, but I'm here today to share my story with ya'll... I was a bully!"

Apple's story was unique and provided additional support for Ms. Benson's reasons of coming forward with her story and wanting to find a solution to the problems facing the people being bullied and those that were the bullies.

After, Apple and Tom-Tom had left Taron in the staircase holding the gun to his head they stepped out of the building to the parking lot. Chester Police were pulling up after getting a report that a student brandished a gun inside the school. The cops leaped out of their cars and told the boys to stop, in order to be searched and investigated for being possible suspects.

Apple and Tom-Tom refused then went for their weapons. The boys didn't have a chance. Chester Police unloaded a barrage of bullets on the group, but only hitting Apple and Tom-Tom. The other boys didn't resist. They immediately raised their hands when ordered by the cops. Tom-Tom was shot six times in the chest, while Apple got hit twice. Once in the chest and the other in his back. The bullet that landed in his back severed Apple's spine. Tom-Tom wasn't lucky. He died at the scene from his wounds. Apple was transported to the hospital and placed under arrest for possessing a weapon. He stayed in the hospital for six months chained to the bed before being taking to prison. The detectives, who were investigating the shooting, interviewed Ms. Benson and the other kids that were in the staircase nobody came forward with any useful information that Apple had brandished a weapon on the kids nor did anybody put a gun in Taron's hand. The police closed the case and Apple was stuck with a firearm charge. Which, he plead guilty to and received probation.

"My friend was killed for our stupid actions of being bullies and this is what led me to being in this wheelchair today..." Apple dropped his head, while reflecting on his past actions and Tom-Tom's death. "I... I..." Apple couldn't continue. Tears started streaming down his face. Cory stepped over and rubbed Apple's back. He reached and took the mic out of Apple's hand then stared at the crowd.

"What, my friend is trying to say is that, being a bully is a serious mistake that has major consequences on everybody involved. That's why we're here today, in order to provide people around the country with a better way to deal with being bullied and those that are bullies. We're launching a free app today that will be helpful to those, who are being bullied and afraid to seek help. The free app will let you provide the name and, or picture of the bully or bullies then it would be dealt with immediately. You would remain anonymous, if that's what you choose to be and, if you're a bully we could provide you with our counseling services, in order to help you with your problems of being a bully and taking advantage of people... But, every claim would be investigated by the Break Free team and, if necessary sent to the proper authorities."

Cory went on explaining about the significance and benefits of the free app. Break Free was making a ground-breaking achievement with introducing a solution to the bully issue going on in America. This app was just the beginning on the battlefront to fight against the bullies. There still was a long way to go before the issue could be solved and Break Free was prepared for the long fight.

Cory completed his speech and waved Ms. Benson over to the pulpit, so she could proceed in hosting the event. The crowd roared and began yelling and screaming, "Break Free! Break Free! Break Free! Break Free!" The Foundation had finally brought some unity to the citizens of Chester and some hope that the City desperately needed. Which, they had been denied for several years.

The End

Final Thoughts

The ideal for the story was brought to me by my two boys, who wanted me to write a short-story about kids playing football and being bullied. Over the course of a couple weeks both of them sent me ideals, then I went ahead and start putting the story into motion. While contemplating on how to frame the story and from which angle to come from I came to realize that the bully issue was not just a kid problem, but an American issue that had no age limit. I thought about the professional football player from the Miami Dolphins, who had been bullied. The kids and, or teenagers that committed suicide because they couldn't handle the pressure of being bullied on the social media networks and other incidents that had been televised over the past years. America still haven't come up with a solution to the problem and this fact had me puzzled. How could the United States with all these great minds living amongst us not have an answer to this very serious dilemma?

It's a great question that we, as Americans, have failed to properly answer. I think now is the time that we make an effort to try and stop this vicious cycle of kids and adults being bullied for nothing other than the fact that they want to be different or that their weaker mentally or physically than the others.

With that being said, I am going to end here and ask that, whoever reads this story and gets a boost of inspiration that you try and make a different. No matter how small it is.

Sincerely,

Andre D. Cooper

Questions For Review

1 Do you think it is okay that a person wants to be different from the rest of the crowd?

2 If you could talk to a bully face-to-face, as Cory did when he spoke to Apple and Tom-Tom, what would you say to that person?

3 Would you have forgave Apple and accepted him into the Break Free Movement after he was a bully first?

4 Do you think that the Break Free Movement should be a reality?

5 Should teachers or people in general be more vigilant in noticing the signs of kids or adults that they're being bullied, or are bullies?

6 What are the signs of a bully?

7 Can a bully be a hero?

8 How much emotional and physical abuse would it take before you would notify the proper authorities

(teachers, parents, boss, manager, police or anybody else that's in the position to help), that you need help from a bully?

9 Why are people afraid to comment freely online or in person about being bullied?

10 Could you be a good person and still be a bully?

11 Do you think that the bully problem will ever come to an end?

ABOUT THE AUTHOR

Andre "Dre" Cooper was born in Wilmington, Delaware on June 24, 1979, where he was birthed into the world by two teenage parents. At 1 year old, Andre moved to Chester, Pennsylvania with his young mother and her family.

Inside the poverty-stricken city of Chester is where Andre saw the most vivid aspects of crime and violence committed by individuals. With that being his upbringing, Andre was also the victim, at times, of bullies and even later bullied others until being arrested and incarcerated at the age of 23.

Once convicted and sent to federal prison, Andre practiced and molded himself into a creative writer. In 2010, Andre self-published his first novel called, The Life We Chose. That was followed by 'The Life We Chose 2' in 2011 and in 2015, Andre released his latest work, which was inspired by actual events, named 'Betrayal of Sinners'.

André "Dre" Cooper

Andre's experience in life, as an American male traversing through the hectic corners of inner city life, helped him in shaping most of his drama driven stories.

Now, Andre is striving to bring some awareness to the bully crisis through his writing and in the process hopes to help in finding a solution to the problem.

www.ingramcontent.com/pod-product-compliance
Lightning Source LLC
Chambersburg PA
CBHW071906020426
42331CB00010B/2688